UNIVERSITY PRESS

World Instruments

Tracey Reeder

Contents

People all around the world make music. They use lots of different instruments.

Bagpipes

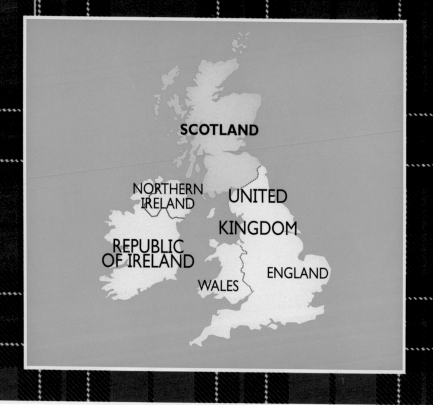

This man is in Scotland. He is blowing into his bagpipes to make music. He has to blow very hard.

Steel Drums

These people are banging on steel drums to make music. These people live in the West Indies. Steel drums are often made from oil drums.

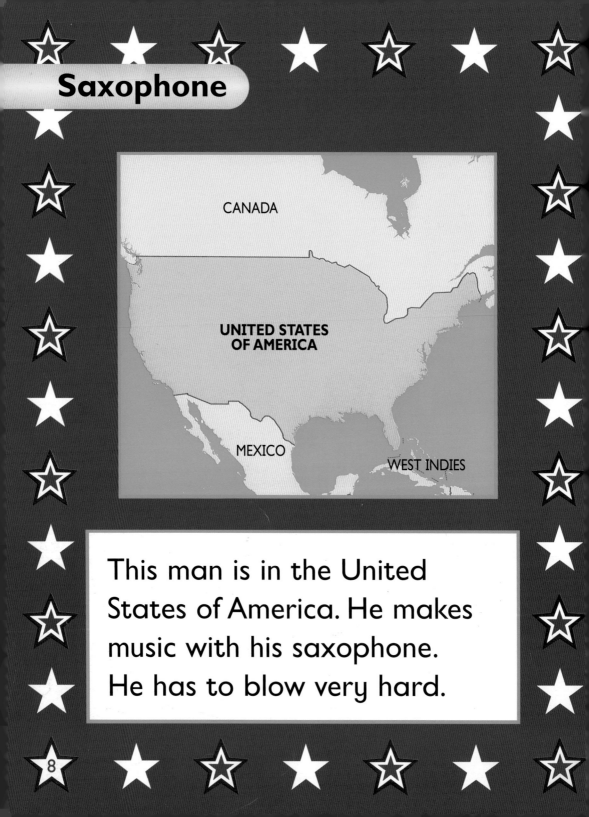

CANADA

UNITED STATES
OF AMERICA

MEXICO

WEST INDIES

This man is in the United States of America. He makes music with his saxophone. He has to blow very hard.

Panpipes

This girl is playing the panpipes. She blows into her panpipes very gently. She makes her music in Peru.

Sitar

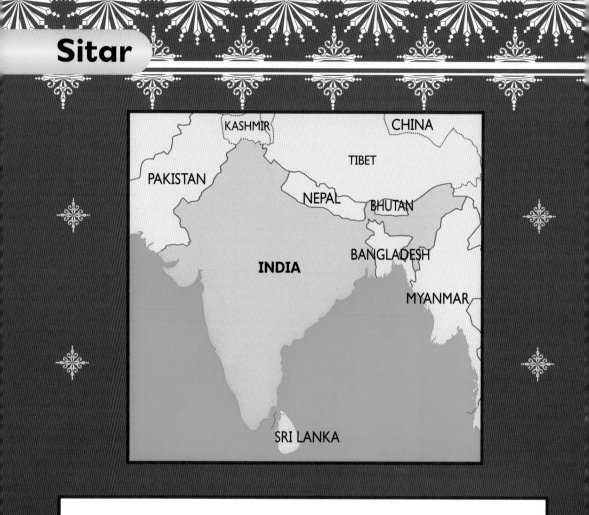

This woman is in India. She is making music with a sitar.

Didgeridoo

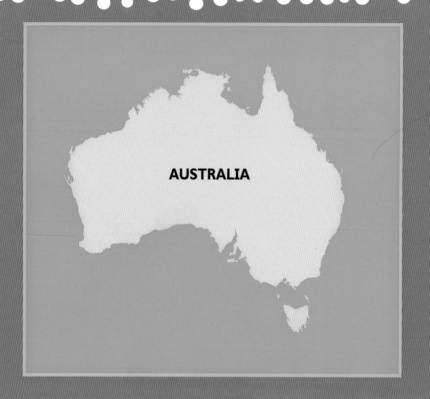

AUSTRALIA

This man is playing a didgeridoo. He has to blow very hard. He lives in Australia.

Index